# JAZZ BALLADS

D1036439

| | |
|---|---|
| 2 | Autumn In New York |
| 7 | Bewitched |
| 10 | Body And Soul |
| 15 | But Beautiful |
| 18 | Can't Help Lovin' Dat Man |
| 26 | Come Rain Or Come Shine |
| 23 | Darn That Dream |
| 28 | God Bless' The Child |
| 32 | Here's That Rainy Day |
| 35 | I Can't Get Started With You |
| 38 | I Concentrate On You |
| 44 | I Didn't Know What Time It Was |
| 46 | I Remember You |
| 41 | I'll Never Smile Again |
| 50 | If I Should Lose You |
| 54 | Imagination |
| 58 | In A Sentimental Mood |
| 64 | It Could Happen To You |
| 61 | June In January |
| 68 | Like Someone In Love |
| 72 | Lover Man (Oh, Where Can You Be?) |
| 76 | Misty |
| 82 | Mood Indigo |
| 86 | Moonlight Becomes You |
| 79 | Moonlight In Vermont |
| 90 | More Than You Know |
| 92 | My Foolish Heart |
| 95 | My Funny Valentine |
| 98 | My Old Flame |
| 102 | My One And Only Love |
| 110 | My Romance |
| 105 | My Silent Love |
| 114 | Nearness Of You, The |
| 122 | Nightingale Sang In Berkeley Square, A |
| 119 | Solitude |
| 126 | Sophisticated Lady |
| 132 | Stella By Starlight |
| 129 | Stormy Weather (Keeps Rainin' All The Time) |
| 136 | Unforgettable |
| 148 | Very Thought Of You, The |
| 138 | When I Fall In Love |
| 140 | You Are Too Beautiful |
| 144 | You Don't Know What Love Is |

ISBN 0-7935-3318-X

HAL•LEONARD™
CORPORATION
7777 W. BLUEMOUND RD. P.O. BOX 13819 MILWAUKEE, WI 53213

# AUTUMN IN NEW YORK

Words and Music by
VERNON DUK[E]

# BEWITCHED
## (From "PAL JOEY")

Words by LORENZ HART
Music by RICHARD RODGERS

He's a fool and don't I know it. But a fool can have his charms.
Love's the same old sad sen-sa-tion. Late-ly I've not slept a wink

I'm in love and don't I show it, Like a babe in arms.
Since this half-pint im-i-ta-tion

Put me on the blink. I'm wild a-gain, Be-guiled a-gain, A

# BODY AND SOUL

Words by EDWARD HEYMAN, ROBERT SOUR and FRANK EYTON
Music by JOHN GREEN

dance to prove, dear. My life a wreck you're mak - ing,

you know I'm yours for just the tak - ing; I'd glad - ly sur -

ren - der my - self to you, bod - y and

soul! soul!

# BUT BEAUTIFUL

Words by JOHNNY BURKE
Music by JIMMY VAN HEUSEN

# CAN'T HELP LOVIN' DAT MAN
## (From "SHOW BOAT")

Lyrics by OSCAR HAMMERSTEIN II
Music by JEROME KERN

# DARN THAT DREAM

Lyric by EDDIE DeLANGE
Music by JIMMY VAN HEUSEN

# COME RAIN OR COME SHINE
## (From "ST. LOUIS WOMAN")

Words by JOHNNY MERCER
Music by HAROLD ARLEN

# GOD BLESS' THE CHILD

Words and Music by ARTHUR HERZOG JR.
and BILLIE HOLIDAY

Them that's got shall get, them that's not shall lose, So the Bi-ble said, and it still is news; Ma-ma may have, Pa-pa may have, but God Bless' the child that's

# HERE'S THAT RAINY DAY

Words by JOHNNY BURKE
Music by JIMMY VAN HEUSEN

# I CAN'T GET STARTED WITH YOU

## (From "ZIEGFELD FOLLIES")

Words by IRA GERSHWIN
Music by VERNON DUKE

# I CONCENTRATE ON YOU

Words and Music by
COLE PORTER

# I'LL NEVER SMILE AGAIN

Words and Music by
RUTH LOWE

# I DIDN'T KNOW WHAT TIME IT WAS
### (From "TOO MANY GIRLS")

Words by LORENZ HART
Music by RICHARD RODGERS

Moderately

# I REMEMBER YOU

### (From The Paramount Picture "THE FLEET'S IN")

Words by JOHNNY MERCER
Music by VICTOR SCHERTZINGER

Was it in Ta - hi - ti? Were we on the

Nile? Long, long a - go, say an hour or so

I re - call that I saw your smile.

# IF I SHOULD LOSE YOU

## (From The Paramount Picture "ROSE OF THE RANCHO")

Words and Music by LEO ROBIN
and RALPH RAINGER

# IMAGINATION

Words by JOHNNY BURKE
Music by JIMMY VAN HEUSEN

8ba⌐

# IN A SENTIMENTAL MOOD

Words and Music by DUKE ELLINGTON,
IRVING MILLS and MANNY KURTZ

**Slowly with expression**

# JUNE IN JANUARY
### (From The Paramount Picture "HERE IS MY HEART")

Words and Music by LEO ROBIN
and RALPH RAINGER

62

# IT COULD HAPPEN TO YOU

## (From The Paramount Picture "AND THE ANGELS SING")

Words by JOHNNY BURKE
Music by JAMES VAN HEUSEN

# LIKE SOMEONE IN LOVE

Words by JOHNNY BURKE
Music by JIMMY VAN HEUSEN

# LOVER MAN

## (OH, WHERE CAN YOU BE?)

By JIMMY DAVIS, ROGER "RAM" RAMIREZ
and JIMMY SHERMAN

MCA music publishing

Dm  G7  Dm  G7

I don't know why, but I'm feel - ing so sad. ___

C9  Gm7  C9  C7  F7#9

I long to try some-thing I've nev - er had, ___ nev - er had no kiss - in'

Bb7  Eb7  Gm7b5  C9  Gm7

oh, what I've been miss - in'. Lov - er man, oh where can you

F  A7  Dm  G7  Dm  G7

be? The night is cold, and I'm so all a - lone, ___

# MISTY

Words by JOHNNY BURKE
Music by ERROLL GARNER

Slowly, with expression

Look at me, I'm as help-less as a kit-ten up a tree And I feel like I'm

cling-ing to a cloud, I can't___ un-der-stand,___ I get mist-y just hold-ing your

hand.___ Walk my way and a

# MOONLIGHT IN VERMONT

Words and Music by JOHN BLACKBURN
and KARL SUESSDORF

Pen - nies in a stream, fall - ing leaves, a sy - ca - more, moon - light in Ver - mont. I - cy fin - ger - waves,

# MOOD INDIGO

Words and Music by DUKE ELLINGTON,
IRVING MILLS and ALBANY BIGARD

# MOONLIGHT BECOMES YOU

**(From The Paramount Picture "ROAD TO MOROCCO")**

Words by JOHNNY BURKE
Music by JAMES VAN HEUSEN

# MORE THAN YOU KNOW

Words by WILLIAM ROSE and EDWARD ELISCU
Music by VINCENT YOUMANS

Slowly, With Expression

# MY FOOLISH HEART

Words by NED WASHINGTON
Music by VICTOR YOUNG

# MY FUNNY VALENTINE
## (From "BABES IN ARMS")

Words by LORENZ HART
Music by RICHARD RODGERS

# MY OLD FLAME

### (From The Paramount Picture "BELLE OF THE NINETIES")

Words and Music by ARTHUR JOHNSTON
and SAM COSLOW

The mu-sic seemed to be so rem-i-nis-cent; I knew I'd heard it some-where be-fore. I racked my re-col-lec-tions as I lis-tened When sud-den-ly I re-mem-bered once more.

# MY ONE AND ONLY LOVE

Words by ROBERT MELLIN
Music by GUY WOOD

# MY SILENT LOVE

Words by EDWARD HEYMAN
Music by DANA SUESSE

# MY ROMANCE
## (From "JUMBO")

Words by LORENZ HART
Music by RICHARD RODGERS

# THE NEARNESS OF YOU
## (From The Paramount Picture "ROMANCE IN THE DARK")

Words by NED WASHINGTON
Music by HOAGY CARMICHAEL

# SOLITUDE

Words and Music by DUKE ELLINGTON,
EDDIE DeLANGE and IRVING MILLS

# A NIGHTINGALE SANG IN BERKELEY SQUARE

Lyric by ERIC MASCHWITZ
Music by MANNING SHERWIN

That cer-tain night, the night we met, there was
strange it was, how sweet and strange, there was

mag-ic a-broad in the air.
nev-er a dream to com-pare

There were an-gels din-ing
with that ha-zy, cra-zy

at the Ritz, and a night-in-gale sang in Ber - k'ley
night we met, when a night-in-gale sang in Ber - k'ley
*Pronounced (Bar - kley)*

as we kissed and said "good - night," a night - in - gale sang in

like an e - cho far a - way, a night - in - gale sang in

Ber - k'ley Square. _____ How

Square. I know 'cause I was there,

that night in Ber - k'ley Square. _____

*8va*

# SOPHISTICATED LADY

Words and Music by DUKE ELLINGTON,
IRVING MILLS and MITCHELL PARISH

# STORMY WEATHER
## (Keeps Rainin' All The Time)

Lyrics by TED KOEHLER
Music by HAROLD ARLEN

Slow lament

Don't know why there's no sun up in the sky, Storm-y Weath-er,

Since my {man/gal} and I ain't to-geth-er, keeps rain-in' all the time.

Life is bare, gloom and mis-'ry ev-'ry-where, Storm-y Weath-er,

# STELLA BY STARLIGHT

(From The Paramount Picture "THE UNINVITED")

Words by NED WASHINGTON
Music by VICTOR YOUNG

Have you seen Stel - la by star - light, stand - ing a - lone, moon in her hair? Have you seen Stel - la by star - light,

# UNFORGETTABLE

Words and Music by
IRVING GORDON

# WHEN I FALL IN LOVE

Words by EDWARD HEYMAN
Music by VICTOR YOUNG

# YOU ARE TOO BEAUTIFUL

(From "HALLELUJAH, I'M A BUM")

Words by LORENZ HART
Music by RICHARD RODGERS

Lyrics:

Like all fools, I be-lieved what I want-ed to be-lieve. _____

My fool-ish heart con - ceived what fool-ish hearts con -

ceive. _____ I thought I found a mir - a - cle, I

# YOU DON'T KNOW WHAT LOVE IS

Words and Music by DON RAYE
and GENE DePAUL

# THE VERY THOUGHT OF YOU

Words and Music by
RAY NOBLE

I don't need your pho-to-graph, _____
I hold you re-spon-si - ble, _____

_____ to keep _ by my bed;
_____ I'll take _ it to law,

Your pic - ture is
I nev - er have

al - ways in ____ my head. _____
felt like this _ be - fore. _____